T0199041

A Christmas In The NICU

AMIRIS SABO

To order additional copies of this book, contact:
Xlibris
844-714-8691
www.Xlibris.com
Orders@Xlibris.com

ISBN: Softcover   978-1-6641-4775-1
         EBook   978-1-6641-4774-4

Print information available on the last page

Rev. date: 12/11/2020

WITH GRATITUDE

I always want, firstly, to thank God because He brought me this far. My child-bearing years have been challenging, to say the least. Secondly, I want to give thanks to my husband and my children for their support in everything I do. My little family is the definition of resilience. It is amazing how we encourage and support each other every day to do better and to help others.

Thank you from the bottom of my heart! This book is specially for the two little boys that made me a mommy. I love you.

I Also want to thank my Editor Berthine Crevecoeur West. More than an Editor, she is a colleague, a mentor and a friend to me. Thank you for always believing in me.

PREFACE

I'm not entirely certain if the motivation for me writing this book was because of inspiration or obligation. I write this book because life in the NICU is hard. Life with preeclampsia is especially hard and I want everyone to know that. Having a baby in the NICU is not like you are on vacation; It's not like having a babysitter, so you can sleep. You are constantly worried for the well-being of your child. Every call from the hospital is a constant reminder that your life is not that of normal parenting life. Every doctor's appointment scares you.

The main reason for writing this book is to give you a glimpse into what parents experience when spending the holidays in the NICU. Braxton was born on October 31, 2018. So, we spent Thanksgiving, Christmas, New Year's Day and nearly Valentine's Day in the NICU, while our 6-year-old, Kareem, was at home. It was really hard to give our 6-year-old the perfect holidays when we were not able to be together as a family. But, we did the best we could. We didn't complain, we just changed some traditions and learned some new ones, as well. When you spend the holidays in the hospital, no matter the reason, you feel lonely even if you are surrounded by caring medical personnel. You just wish you were home with your family.

I also wanted to write about the reason why prematurity is part of my life, as this book is the second part of the journey that began with my previous book *From My NICU Window*; which highlighted my son Kareem's story and how preeclampsia had forever changed my life. I wish I could tell you all of the moments God had saved me from death when trying to have a baby. He performed so many miracles to keep me in the world and to give me the most beautiful family. I hope that our story can give you or someone you love the comfort to remember that you are not alone.

OUR JOURNEY

This is the continuation of my story detailed in the book *From My NICU Window*. When I wrote *From My NICU Window*, I had been pregnant four times; My first baby was a stillbirth at 20 weeks, though I was pregnant for 27 weeks. We realize now that I had preeclampsia with that baby. 5 months after that stillbirth, I had a six-week miscarriage; Then in 2011, we had a little girl who was born at 26 weeks and passed away in the NICU when she was 4 days old. She weighed one pound and was extremely premature. In 2013, we had Kareem, our miracle rainbow baby! He was born at 30 weeks and spent 53 days in the NICU. The main reason for all of this prematurity and death has one name, PREECLAMPSIA, which we would come to know as one of the leading causes of prematurity and infant mortality.

During the summer of 2018, I started to feel very tired. At the time I was working 40 hours a week on my feet. I assumed the reason for my extreme fatigue and elevated blood pressure was caused by this strenuous work. But, that wasn't the reason. In June 2018, we found out that I was pregnant with baby #5. We were scheduled to travel to Europe for a month in the next two days. At this point we didn't know what to do. Should we stay or should we go? Anxiety quickly set in. I knew that my life was going to change yet again. I knew that I would have to stay in bed for months. This time, I had to manage this, while being a mother to my 5 year-old kid.

We decide to go to Europe and it was the best vacation ever! When we came back, I went to bed as much as I could. But, between my 5 year-old activities and my weekly doctor appointments, I was exhausted. At 25 weeks, the doctor told me that I could hold my baby shower. (This was going to be the first one we could have, as we were never able to do a proper baby shower or have a pregnancy photoshoot). We had the baby shower at 25 weeks gestation. At 26 weeks, while we were doing the photoshoot, my headache began. I looked at myself in the camera and I saw a different person: my face and my entire body were so very swollen! I knew that I had to listen to my body! That same week, I went to the doctor. At that point, I could not move my head – even that was extremely painful. My doctor and I both knew it was time. Braxton was born on October 31, 2018. He was 27 weeks, 2.8 pounds and 14 inches long. He was in the NICU for 95 days: Christmas, New Year's Day and nearly spent Valentine's Day there, as well. Due to his prematurity, he had lung disease, PDA (Patent Ductus Arteriosus - a persistent opening between the two major blood vessels leading from the heart, which they repaired in the NICU), and an ASD (Atrial Septal Defect - a hole in the wall between the upper chambers of the right and left atria of the heart). We are waiting until he turns 3 years old for this to close or have an open heart surgery.

Within the first 20 months of his life, he has also endured three mayor surgeries: the PDA repair and two inguinal hernia repairs. We were so blessed that there were *only* three surgeries. We are so proud of our little warrior and we are happy to be able to share our story with you!

Spending the holidays in the NICU was certainly an experience! But, we made the best of it and we want to share a little bit of what happened one special Christmas in the NICU at Gwinnet Medical Center in Georgia (USA).

SOME FACTS ABOUT PREECLAMPSIA:

- Preeclampsia is a disorder that occurs during both pregnancy and the postpartum period. It affects both the mother and the unborn baby. Affecting at least 5-8% of all pregnancies, it its characterized by high blood pressure and oftentimes, the presence of protein in the urine

- Early recognition of preeclampsia symptoms can save your life

- 1 in 12 pregnancies are at risk

- 40% of necessary preterm deliveries are due to preeclampsia

- 75% of postpartum maternal deaths are associated with preeclampsia after delivery

- 76,000 maternal deaths and 500,000 infant deaths are attributed to preeclampsia every year

WARNING SIGNS OF PREECLAMPSIA:

- High blood pressure

- Protein in your urine

- Swelling (edema)

- Persistent Headache

- Nausea or vomiting

- Abdominal (stomach area) and shoulder pain

- Lower back pain

- Sudden weight gain

- Changes in vision

- Hyperreflexia (when your reflexes are so strong that your knee jerks back violently when tapped by a rubber hammer)

- Shortness of breath

- Anxiety

ADVICE FROM A PREECLAMPSIA SURVIVOR

It is important to listen to your body and check for warning signs. Being aware of warning signs doesn't mean that you are paranoid. You don't need to experience all of these symptoms. Sometimes, the signs may be silent - like high blood pressure. (It is called the Silent Killer for a reason.) Always remember that you are your baby's advocate, so fight for them always! This means ensuring that your doctors listen to you (especially when they disagree with you), staying in the hospital when necessary and following your doctors recommendations, such as staying in bed, taking your meds or going to the emergency room if you are feeling very ill. Remember, that it is always better to be safe than sorry! Everyone usually has some sort of advice on what you should and shouldn't do when you are pregnant. But, the best advice you can take is that of your doctors and you listening to your body. Never forget that you are not alone! There are a lot of groups for all kinds of pregnancy problems. The Preeclampsia Foundation is ready and willing to provide you with all the help and information that you need.

YOUR NICU HOLIDAY PICTURE

A CHRISTMAS IN THE NICU

A blessed December, a month to remember
A month of great joy, of presents galore,

A month when we celebrate the greatest birth of all,

The birth of baby Jesus Christ.

…And then there was an unexpected surprise, as you, our treasure, had too early arrived.

A baby in the NICU was all that we had.

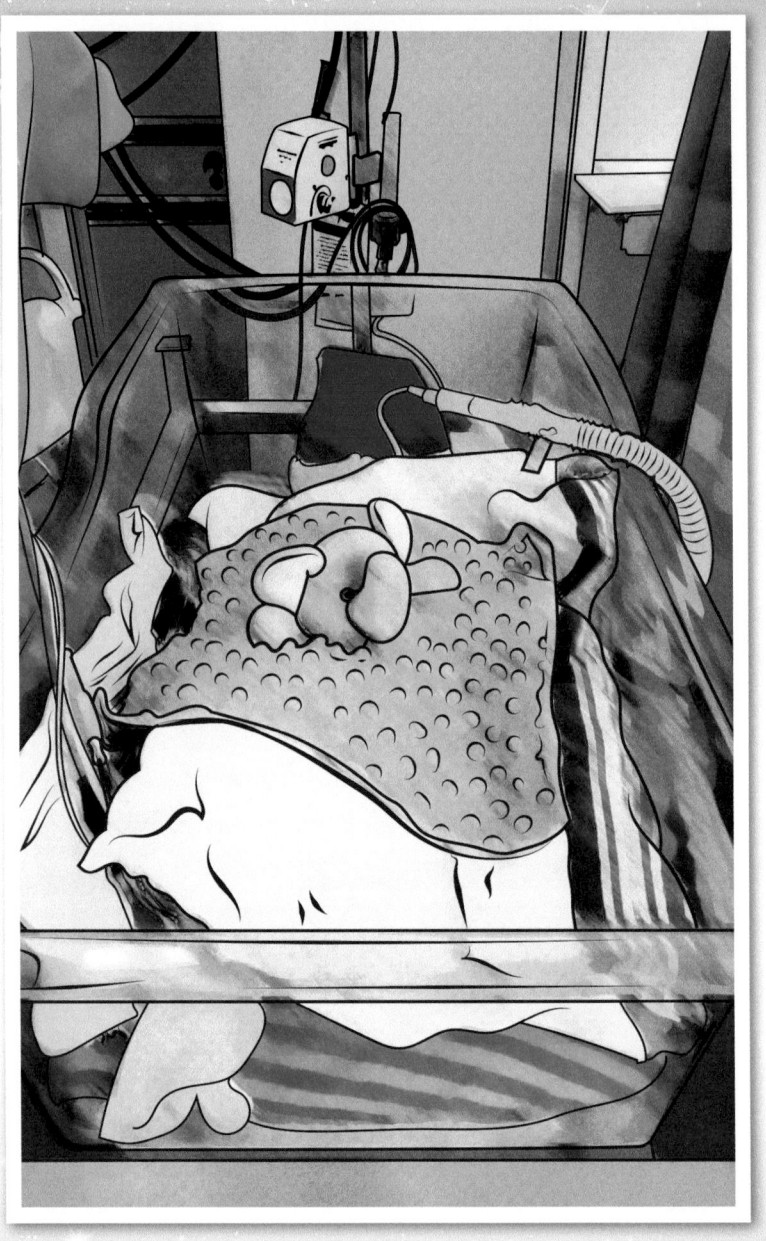

It was Christmas Day, when miracles happen; When wishes
come true and we don't know how they happen.

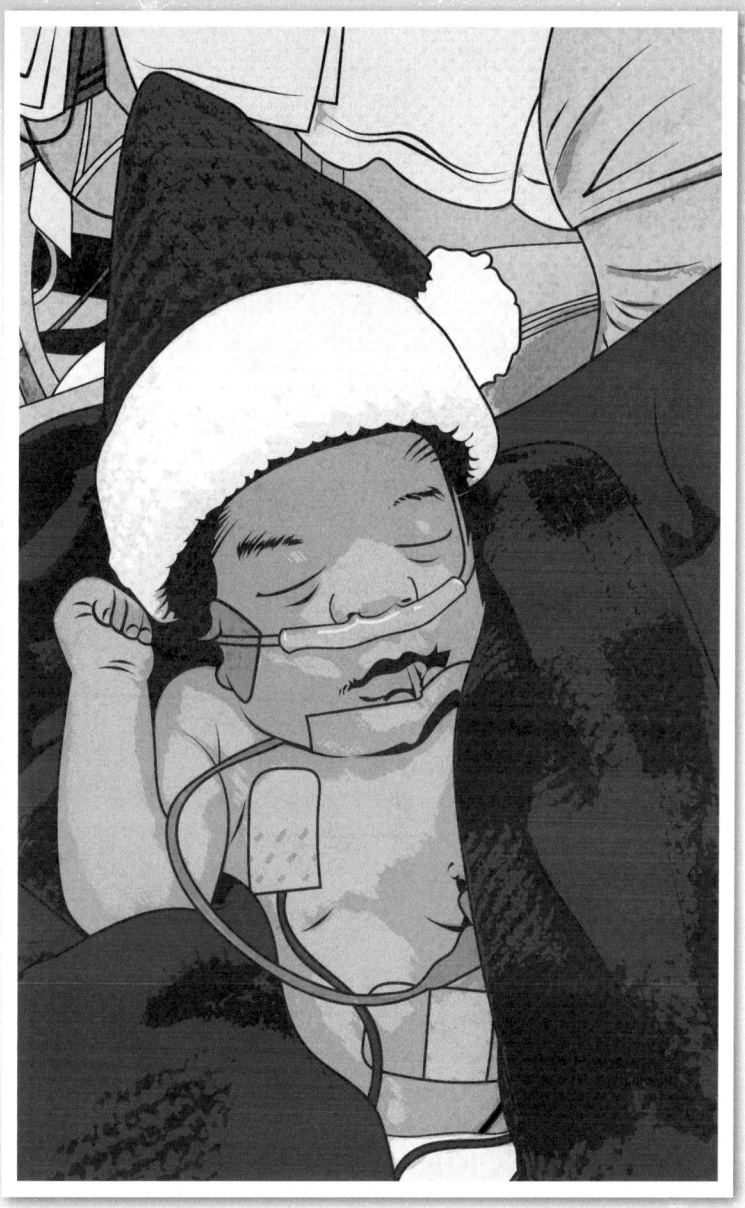

It was Christmas Day and in the NICU we were; Blessed
with ten little fingers perfect in every way.

It was Christmas Day and in the NICU we were; Wondering what gift he could actually wear.
Pajamas were tiny and no need was for them. The chimney was missing but the lights were all there.

It was Christmas Day and in the NICU we were. When all of a sudden, we saw a white beard. It
was Santa Claus with his beautiful wife that had come to the NICU where the miracles are!

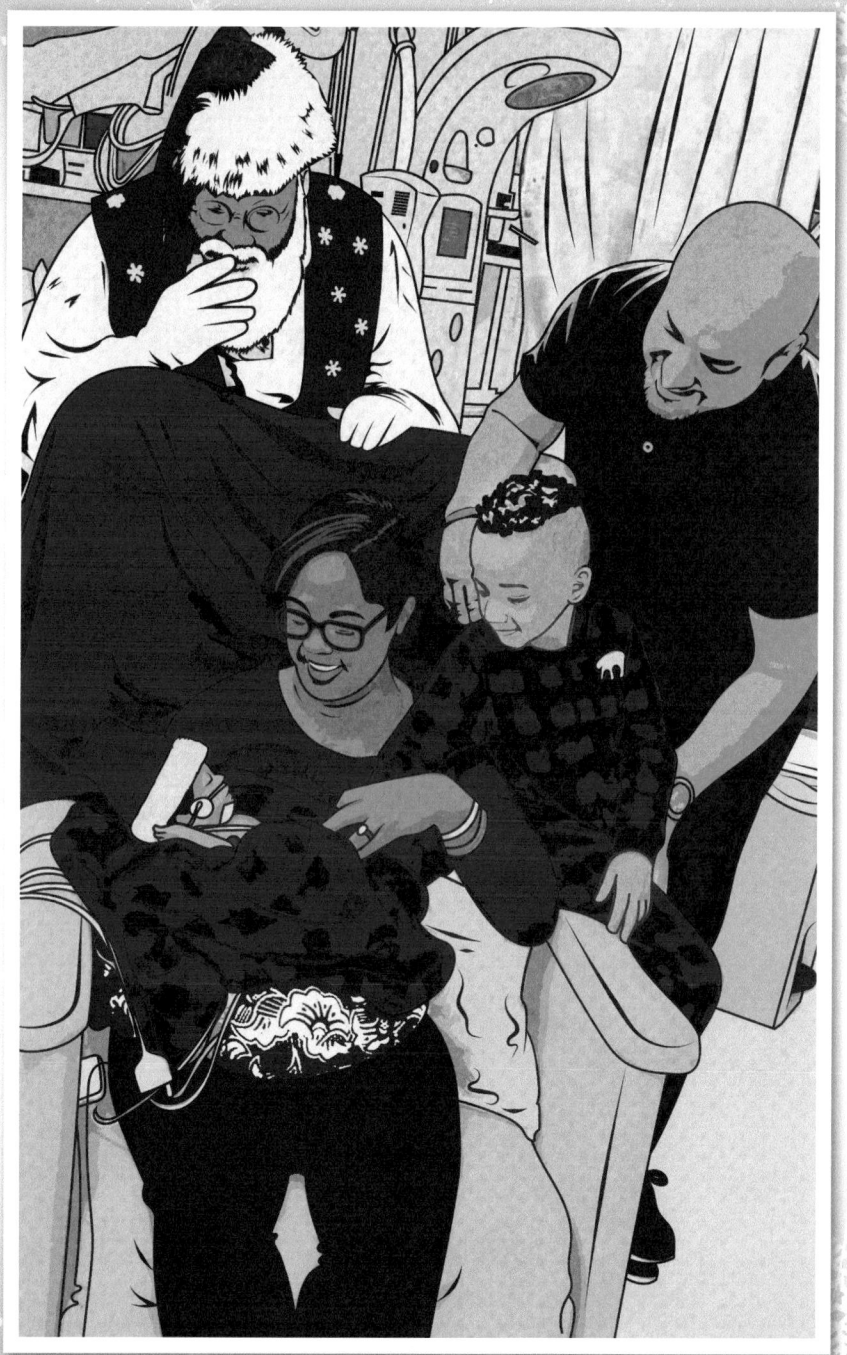

Happy ❄ Holidays
From our family to yours